www.gardenpublishingco.com

Copyright ©2018 by Coy Taylor
Published by Garden Publishing Company LLC
For more information, please visit gardenpublishingco.com

All rights reserved. No parts of this publication may be reproduced, stored in a retrieval system, or transmitted in any form or by any means, electronic, mechanical, photocopying, recording, or otherwise, without the prior written permission of the copyright owner.

This book is sold subject to the condition that it shall not, by way of trade or otherwise, be lent, resold, hired out, or otherwise circulated without the publisher's prior consent in any form of binding or cover other than that in which it is published and without a similar condition including this condition being imposed on the subsequent purchaser. Under no circumstances may any part of this book be photocopied for resale.

ISBN-10: 1987526597
ISBN-13: 978-1987526592

Cover design by Garden Publishing Co.
Interior design by Garden Publishing Co.

Printed in the United States of America.

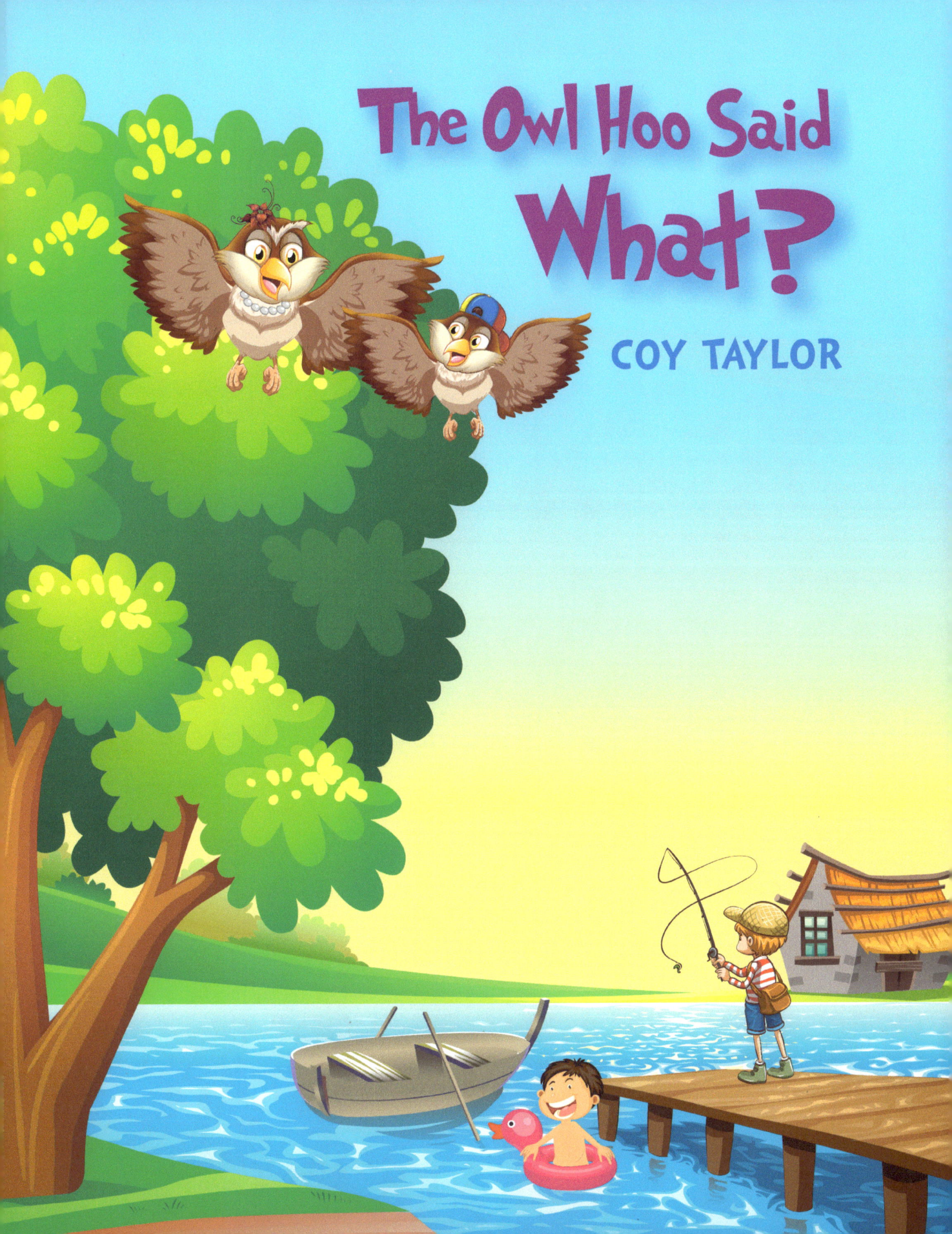

Dedication

I dedicate this book to my beautiful wife, Kristi, and my two wonderful daughters, Allie and Mattie. I'll never forget the morning this all came together over coffee and laughter. You three are the light of my life.

Note to the Reader

This is a work of fiction. Names, characters, businesses, places, events, locales, and incidents are either the products of the author's imagination or used in a fictitious manner. Any resemblance to actual persons, living or dead, or actual events is purely coincidental.

Once upon a time in a wooded forest lived Baby Owl and his mother, Florence. Florence was wise as wise could be while Baby Owl was just starting his ABC's.

Today as they flew from tree to tree, Baby Owl had many questions for his mother, you and me.

What? What? What is that?
That is a school, Mama Owl said.

A School? Yes, a school.

A school is where you go to
study and learn,
make many new friends
and always take turns.

What? What? What is that?
That is a library, Mama Owl said.

A library? Yes, a library.

A library is a building filled with every kind of book. You can learn about anything, even how to cook.

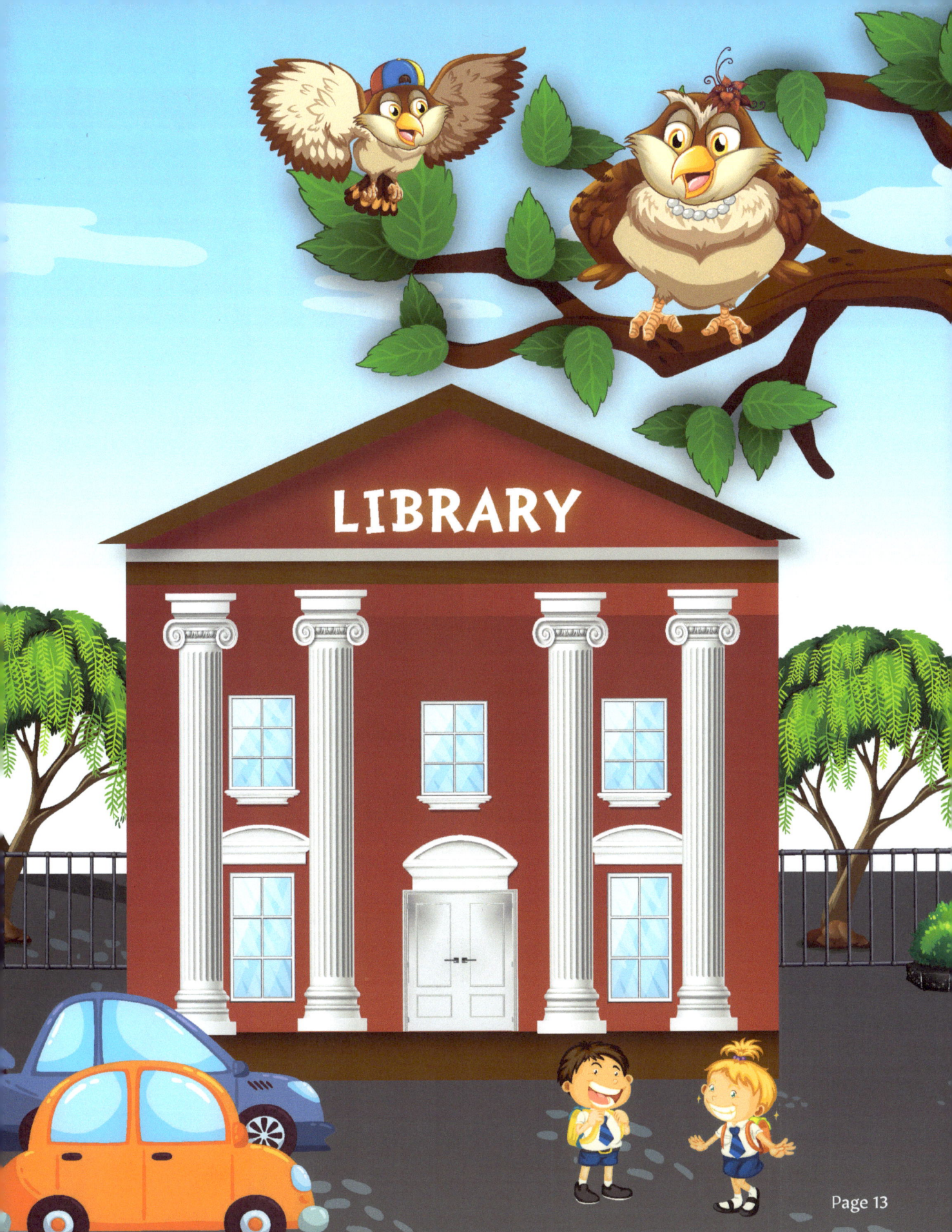

What? What? What is that?
That is a bus, Mama Owl said.

A bus? Yes, a bus.

A bus is like a car,
but quite a bit bigger.
It holds many more people but
it's definitely not quicker.

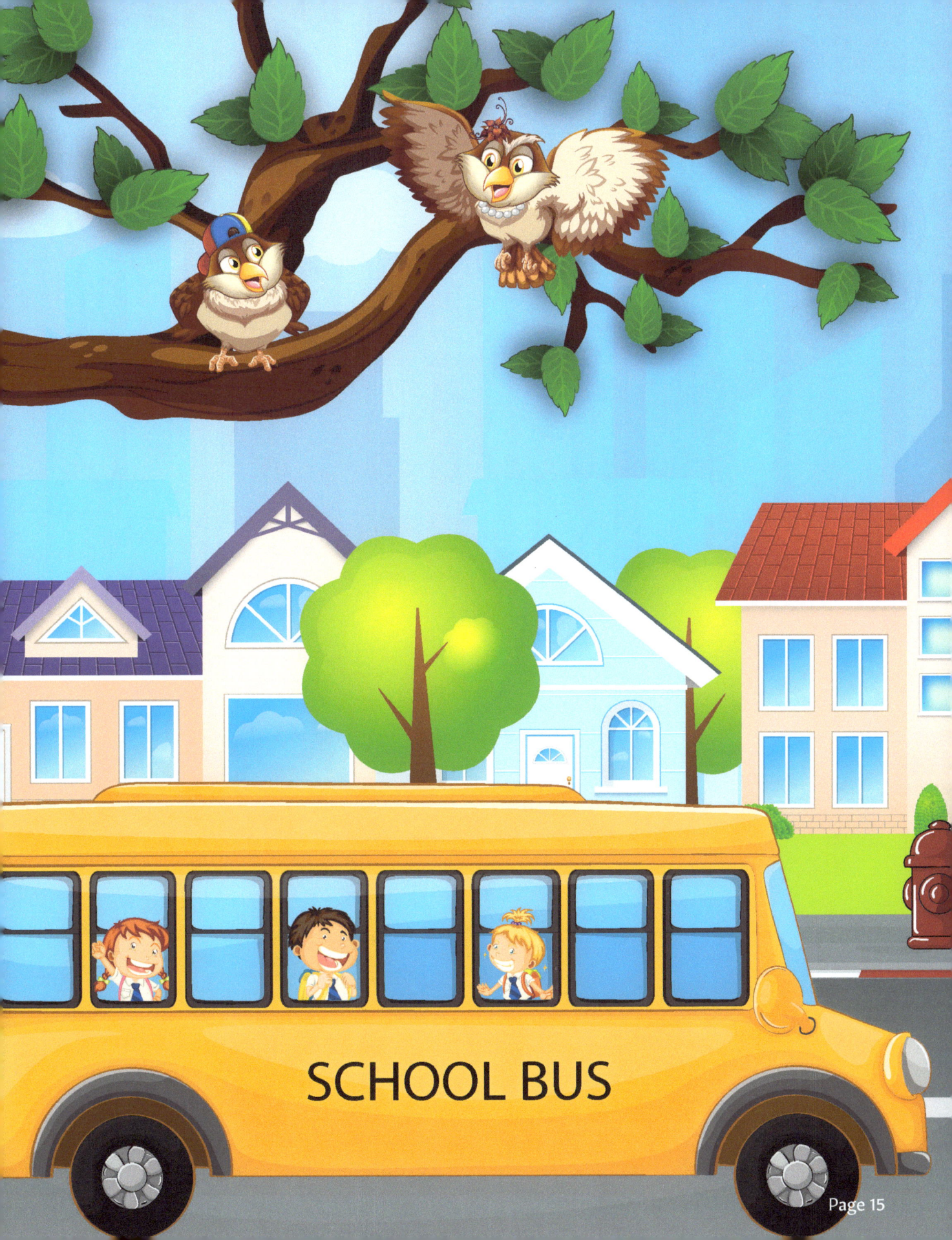

What? What? What is that?
That is a farm, Mama Owl said.

A farm? Yes, a farm.

A farm is where animals like cows and chickens make milk and eggs
you use in the kitchen. It's where farmers grow vegetables, fruits and more to sell at the market and grocery stores.

What? What? What is that?
That is a lake, Mama Owl said.

A lake? Yes, a lake.

A lake is where there's plenty of water,
and where people go when it gets hotter.
Fishing, skiing and swimming for fun
all at the lake under the sun.

What? What? What is that?
That is a city, Mama Owl said.

A city? Yes, a city.

A city is where people live, work and play. There are many big buildings, parks and even churches for them to pray.

What? What? What is that?
That is a zoo, Mama Owl said.

A zoo? Yes, a zoo.

A zoo is filled with lots of animals,
all different shapes, sizes and colors.
People go to see them from all over the
world, fathers, sons, mothers and daughters.

Now that the day is over and ending many questions answered it's time to start spending the rest of the evening flying home to start tending to making our beds for spending the night.

Good night, my precious one.

About the Author

Coy Taylor loves to fish, laugh, and spend time with his family watching the West Texas sunsets. Reading children's books and telling stories to his kids was one of his favorite things to do. He lives in Midland, Texas, with his wife Kristi and their two daughters, and cannot wait for grandchildren.

Upcoming Titles by Coy Taylor

The Owl Hoo Said, Where?
The Owl Hoo Said, When?
The Owl Hoo Said, Why?
The Owl Hoo Finally Said, Who?

www.ingramcontent.com/pod-product-compliance
Lightning Source LLC
Chambersburg PA
CBHW040758240426
43673CB00014B/387